PROFILES IN FATHERHOOD

THE BIBLE LESSONS OF JOHN QUINCY ADAMS FOR HIS SON

THE VISION FORUM, INC.
San Antonio, Texas

Dedicated to my father, Howard Phillips,
who read the Bible to me, both Old and New Testaments,
most every night at our dinner table.

OTHER BOOKS FROM VISION FORUM

PUBLISHER'S INTRODUCTION TO THE 2000 EDITION

In 1800, President Thomas Jefferson commissioned a national survey conducted by Dupont de Numours to determine the status of literacy in America. The results were phenomenal. Better than ninety-seven percent of American citizens could read and write. The stated reason for this success was that, from Boston to Atlanta, American fathers practiced daily Bible reading with their children around the breakfast table. Long before the creation of government schools or the National Education Association, faithful fathers proved that the simple act of teaching the Holy Scriptures to their children at home would lead our nation to become the most literate in the world.

Two hundred years after the Jefferson survey, there is a growing realization in this nation, especially within the Christian community, that the State should not and cannot raise our children. Of course, this comes as no surprise to those parents who have read and believed the law of God.

God's Word actually charges parents, not the State, and not even parent-surrogates called school teachers, with the responsibility to train their children in a world and life system that incorporates academic excellence, spiritual wisdom, character training, covenant keeping, and multi-generational faithfulness.

John Quincy Adams was himself the product of a family which embraced this truth. Though Adams did receive superior formal education, his character, his vision and his worldview were largely shaped by his own father, President John Adams, who gave his son not only personal instruction, but opportunities while still a youth, to venture into the world of men, ideas, and action. Consequently, we see young John Quincy officially serving his country in the Court of France at the age of fourteen. Remarkable!

Modern fathers have come to accept as normative the idea that the sum of their involvement in the life of a boy is attendance at a few athletic events and the occasional chat. Some surveys indicate that, on average, the American father spends a maximum of six minutes a day with his son. The absence of fathers in the life of their sons, coupled with the relegation of spiritual matters to the domain of womanhood, have rendered us a nation populated by fatherless families. And a nation of fatherless families is a dying nation. Perhaps this tendency is why the Bible, in the very last verse of the Old Testament, links true revival to the turning of the hearts of fathers to their sons.

This is why I am fascinated by the story of John Quincy Adams. Here is a man who, in many respects, personifies multi-generational faithfulness. First as a son, and later as a father, John Quincy Adams enjoyed a life in which parent-directed Christian discipleship was paramount.

As to content, I must honestly admit that there are aspects of both his theology and political theory which concern me. Some of those concerns, the theological in particular, will become apparent to the Evangelical reader who peruses the following letters of our former president. It is important to note, however, that John Quincy Adams lived and wrote these letters at a time when the orthodox Christianity so beautifully communicated by the Puritans for almost two centuries was under savage attack from Unitarianism. As early as 1800, many of the universities and churches established to preach the Gospel had abandoned their rich Reformation heritage for the new anti-Trinitarian rationalism.

However, these letters of John Quincy Adams reflect a man, who while not completely unaffected by the liberalism of his day, desperately wanted to communicate to his son a love and reverence for Holy Scripture as the Word of God. Regretfully, at points he deviates from an historical and orthodox view of the Bible, as when he questions the literal record of the creation week found in Genesis One. In this respect, Mr. Adams is guilty of the same rationalism that plagues so many modern Evangelical churches and seminaries. But rather than edit these portions of his letters, we have left them intact so that you, the reader, can appreciate the mind of an imperfect, but remarkable man who loved his son and who, even when traveling, took the time to shepherd him.

This book is important, not for the substance of the theology presented, but because it is a record of a very busy man who did not allow his public responsibilities to detract from his fatherly obligations. We must honestly admit that even among the greatest proponents of biblical orthodoxy today, there are precious few who as eloquently and passionately communicate a love for Holy Scripture to their children as did John Quincy Adams to his son.

There are fewer still who would take the time to write nine thoughtful letters to a son exhorting him to be a student of Scripture. Here is a true model of faithful fatherhood. This is why Vision Forum is pleased to bring you these remarkable letters. They, and the appended 1840 poem by Adams, serve as an inspiration to any father who would embrace with gusto the mission of discipling his children.

Douglas W. Phillips, Esq.
Publisher
San Antonio, Texas

ORIGINAL PUBLISHER'S INTRODUCTION

John Quincy Adams, the writer of the following Letters, is widely known as one of the purest and most eminent men of our age. Born in 1767, during the fierce and absorbing discussions of the rights and responsibilities of rulers which heralded our Revolution and war of Independence, he entered his country's service, while yet a mere lad, as secretary to the Russian embassy, and remained through life, with few and brief intermissions, a public servant, filling successively the posts of secretary, ambassador, United States senator, negotiator of the last treaty of peace with Great Britain, secretary of state, president, and finally representative in congress, which station he filled from 1831 to the hour of his death, which took place in the Capitol, February 23, 1848, he having been stricken down with paralysis, while in the act of rising to address the house, two days before; having lived more than eighty years, and passed nearly or quite three fourths of his days in public stations. Though naturally reserved and diffident in manner, and never in the obvious sense a popular man—for his life was devoted to serving rather than pleasing his countrymen—he was profoundly and generally esteemed for his fearless conscientiousness, his ardent patriotism, his vast and various acquirements, and his unfaltering devotion to human freedom. The funeral honors paid to his memory have had no parallel in this country, except in the case of Washington. Those who had seen fit to oppose his election and to defeat his re-election as president, and to whom he had generally stood opposed in party differences, seemed to vie with his warmest supporters in rendering homage to his memory.

The following letters were written by Mr. Adams, while ambassador at St. Petersburg, to one of his sons, who was at school in Massachusetts. Their purpose is the inculcation of a love and reverence for the Holy Scriptures, and a delight in their perusal and study. Throughout his long life, Mr. Adams was himself a daily and devout reader of the Scriptures, and delighted in comparing and considering them in the various languages with which he was familiar, hoping thereby to acquire a nicer and clearer appreciation of their meaning. The Bible was emphatically his counsel and monitor through life, and the fruits of its guidance are seen in the unsullied character which he bore through the turbid waters of political contention to his final earthly rest. Though long and fiercely opposed and contemned in life, he left no man behind him who would wish to fix a stain on the name he has inscribed so high on the roll of his country's most gifted and illustrious sons.

The intrinsic value of these letters, their familiar and

lucid style, their profound and comprehensive views, their candid and reverent spirit, must win for them a large measure of the public attention and esteem. But, apart from even this, the testimony so unconsciously borne [*sic*] by their pure-minded and profoundly learned author to the truth and excellence of the Christian faith and records, will not be lightly regarded. It is no slight testimonial to the verity and worth of Christianity, that in all ages since its promulgation, the great mass of those who have risen to eminence by their profound wisdom, integrity, and philanthropy, have recognized and reverenced in Jesus of Nazareth, the Son of the living God. To the names of Augustine, Xavier, Fenelon, Milton, Newton, Locke, Lavater, Howard, Chateaubriand, and their thousands of compeers in Christian faith, among the world's wisest and noblest, it is not without pride that the American may add, from among his countrymen, those of such men as Washington, Jay, Patrick Henry and John Quincy Adams.

LETTER I

St. Petersburg, Sept., 1811

My Dear Son: In your letter of the 18th January to your mother, you mentioned that you read to your aunt a chapter in the Bible or a section of Doddridge's Annotations every evening. This information gave me real pleasure; for so great is my veneration for the Bible, and so strong my belief, that when duly read and meditated on, it is of all books in the world, that which contributes most to make men good, wise, and happy—that earlier my children begin to read it, the more steadily they pursue the practice of reading it throughout their lives, the more lively and confident will be my hopes that they will prove useful citizens to their country, respectable members of society, and a real blessing to their parents. But I hope you have now arrived at an age to understand that reading, even in the Bible, is a thing in itself, neither good nor bad, but that all the good which can be drawn from it, is by the use and improvement of what you have read, with the help of your own reflection. Young people sometimes boast of how many books, and how much they have read; when, instead of boasting, they ought to be ashamed of having wasted so much time, to so little profit.

I advise you, my son, in whatever you read, and most of all in reading the Bible, to remember that it is for the purpose of making you wiser and more virtuous. I have myself, for many years made it a practice to read through the Bible once every year. I have always endeavored to read it with the same spirit and temper of mind, which I now recommend to you: that is, with the intention and desire that it may contribute to my advancement in wisdom and virtue. My desire is indeed very imperfectly successful; for, like you, and like the Apostle Paul, "I find a law in my members, warring against the laws of my mind." But as I know that it is my nature to be imperfect, so I know that it is my duty to aim at perfection; and feeling and deploring my own frailties, I can only pray Almighty God, for the aid of his Spirit to strengthen my good desires, and to subdue my propensities to evil; for it is from him, that every good and every perfect gift descends. My custom is, to read four or five chapters every morning, immediately after rising from my bed. It employs about an hour of my time, and seems to me the most suitable manner of beginning the day. But, as other cares, duties, and occupations, engage the remainder of it, I have perhaps never a sufficient portion of my time in meditation, upon what I have read. Even meditation itself is often fruitless, unless it has some special object in view; useful thoughts often arise in the mind, and pass away without being remembered or applied to any good purpose—like the seed scattered upon the surface of the ground, which the birds devour, or the wind blows away, or which rot without taking root, however good the soil may be upon which they are cast. We are all, my dear George, unwilling to confess our own faults, even to ourselves: and when our own consciences are too honest to conceal them from us, our self-love is always busy, either in attempting to disguise them to us under false and delusive colors, or in seeking out excuses and apologies to reconcile them to our minds. Thus, although I am sensible that I have not derived from my assiduous perusal of the Bible (and I might apply the same remark to almost everything else that I do) all the benefit that I might and ought, I am as constantly endeavoring to persuade myself that it is not my own fault. Sometimes I say to myself, I do not understand what I have read; I can not help it; I did not make my own understanding: there are many things in the Bible "hard to understand," as St. Peter expressly says of Paul's epistles: some are hard in the Hebrew, and some in the Greek—the original languages in which the Scriptures were written; some are harder still in the translations. I have been obliged to lead a wandering life about the world, and scarcely ever have at hand the book, which might help me to surmount these difficulties. Conscience sometimes puts the question—whether my not understanding many passages is not owing to my want of attention in reading them. I must admit, that it is; a full proof of which is, that every time I read the Book through, I understand some passages which I never understood before, and which I should have done, at a former reading, had it been affected with a sufficient degree of attention. Then, in answer to myself, I say; it is true; but I can not always command my own attention, and never can to the degree that I wish. My mind is oftentimes so full of other things, absorbed in bodily pain, or engrossed by passion, or distracted by pleasure, or exhausted by dissipation, that I can not give to proper daily employment the attention which I gladly would, and which is absolutely necessary to make it "fruitful of good works." This acknowledgment of my weakness is just; but for how much of it I am still accountable to God, I hardly dare acknowledge to myself. Is it Bodily pain? How often was that brought upon me by my own imprudence or folly? Was it passion? Heaven has given to every human being, the power of controlling his passions, and if he neglects or loses it, the fault is his own, and he must be answerable for it. Was it pleasure? Why did I indulge it? Was it dissipation? This is the most inexcusable of all; for it must have been occasioned by my own thoughtlessness or irresolution. It is of no use to discover our own fault and infirmities, unless the discovery prompts us to amendment.

I have thought if in addition to the hour which I daily give to the reading of the Bible, I should also from time to time (and especially on the Sabbath) apply another hour occasionally to communicate to you the reflection that arise in my mind upon its perusal, it might not only tend to fix and promote my own attention to the excellent instructions of that sacred Book, but perhaps also assist your advancement in its knowledge and wisdom. At your age, it is probable that you have still greater difficulties to understand all that you read in the Bible, than I have at mine; and if you have so much self-observation as your letters indicate, you will be sensible of as much want of attention, both voluntary and involuntary, as I here acknowledge in myself. I intend, therefore, for the purpose of contribution to your improvement and my own, to write you several letters, in due time to follow this, in which I shall endeavor to show you how you may derive the most advantage to yourself, from the perusal of the Scriptures. It is probable, when you receive these letters, you will not, at first reading entirely understand them; if that should be the case, ask your grand-parents, or your uncle or aunt, to explain them: if you still find them too hard, put them on file, and lay them by for two or three years, after which read them again, and you will find them easy enough. It is essential, my son, in order that you may go through life with comfort to yourself, and usefulness to your fellow-creatures, that you should form and adopt certain rules or principles, for the government of your own conduct and temper. Unless you have such rules and principles, there will be numberless occasion on which you will have no guide for your government but your passions. In your infancy and youth, you have been, and will be for some years, under the authority and control of your friends and instructors; but you must soon come to the age when you must govern yourself. You have already come to that age in many respects; you know that difference between right and wrong, and you know some of your duties, and the obligation you are under, to become acquainted with them all. It is in the Bible, you must learn them, and from the Bible how to practice them. Those duties are to God, to your fellow creatures, and to yourself. "Thou shalt love the

Lord thy god, with all thy heart, and with all thy soul, and with all thy mind, and with all thy strength, and thy neighbor as thyself." On these two commandments, Jesus Christ expressly says, "hang all the law and the prophets;" that is to say, the whole purpose of Divine Revelation is to inculcate them efficaciously upon the minds of men. You will perceive that I have spoken of duties to yourself, distinct from those to God and to your fellow-creatures; while Jesus Christ speaks only of two commandments. The reason is, because Christ, and the commandments repeated by him, consider self-love as so implanted in the heart of every man by the law of his nature, that it requires no commandment to establish its influence over the heart; and so great do they know its power to be, that they demand no other measure for the love of our neighbor, than that which they know we shall have for ourselves. But from the love of God, and the love of our neighbor, result duties to ourselves as well as to them, and they are all to be learned in equal perfection by our searching the Scriptures.

Let us, then, search the Scriptures; and, in order to pursue our inquiries with methodical order, let us consider the various sources of information, that we may draw from in this study. The Bible contains the revelation of the will of God. It contains the history of the creation of the world, and of mankind; and afterward the history of one peculiar nation, certainly the most extraordinary nation that has ever appeared upon the earth. It contains a system of religion, and of morality, which we may examine upon its own merits, independent of the sanction it receives from being the Word of God; and it contains a numerous collection of books, written at different ages of the world, by different authors, which we may survey as curious monuments of antiquity, and as literary compositions. In what light so ever we regard it, whether with reference to revelation, to literature, to history, or to morality—it is an invaluable and inexhaustible mine of knowledge and virtue. I shall number separately those letters that I mean to write you upon the subject of the Bible, and as, after they are finished, I shall perhaps ask you to read them all together, or to look over them again myself, you must keep them on separate file. I wish that hereafter they may be useful to your brothers and sisters, as well as to you. As you will receive them as a token of affection for you, during my absence, I pray that they may be worthy to read by them all with benefit to themselves, if it please God, that they should live to be able to understand them.

From your affectionate Father,

JOHN QUINCY ADAMS

LETTER II

The first point of view in which I have invited you to consider the Bible, is in the light of Divine Revelation. And what are we to understand by these terms? I intend as much as possible, to avoid the field of controversy, which I am not well acquainted with, and for which I have little respect, and still less inclination. My idea of the Bible as a Divine Revelation, is founded upon its practical use to mankind, and not upon metaphysical subtleties. There are three points of doctrine, the belief of which, forms the foundation of all morality. The first is, the existence of a God; the second is the immortality of the human soul; and the third is, a future state of rewards and punishments. Suppose it possible for a man to disbelieve either of these articles of faith, and that man will have no conscience, he will have no other law than that of the tiger or the shark; the laws of man may bind him in chains, or may put him to death, but they never can make him wise, virtuous, or happy. It is possible to believe them all without believing that the Bible is a Divine revelation. It is so obvious to every reasonable being, that he did not make himself, and the world which he inhabits, could as little make itself, that the moment we begin to exercise the power of reflection, it seems impossible to escape the conviction that there is a Creator. It is equally evident that the Creator must be a spiritual, and not a material being; there is also a consciousness that the thinking part of our nature is not material, but spiritual—that it is not subject to the laws of matter, nor perishable with it. Hence arises the belief, that we have an immortal soul; and pursuing the train of thought which the visible creation and observation upon ourselves suggest, we must soon discover that the Creator must also be the Governor of the universe; that his wisdom, and his goodness, must be without bounds—that he is a righteous God, and loves righteousness—that mankind are bound by the laws of righteousness, and are accountable to him for their obedience to them in this life, according to their good or evil deeds. This completion of Divine justice must be reserved for another life. The existence of a Creator, the immortality of the human soul, and a future state of retribution, are therefore so perfectly congenial to natural reason when once discovered—or rather it is so impossible for natural reason to disbelieve them—that it would seem the light of natural reason could alone suffice for their discovery; but the conclusion would not be correct. Human reason may be sufficient to get an obscure glimpse of these sacred and important truths, but it can not discover them, in all their clearness. For example;—in all their numberless, false religions, which have swayed the minds of men in different ages, and regions of the world, the idea of a God has always been included:

"Father of all! In every age,
In every clime adored—
By saint, by savage, and by sage—
Jehovah, Jove, or Lord."

So says Pope's Universal Prayer. But, it is the God of the Hebrews alone, who is announced to us as the Creator of the world. The ideas of God entertained by all the most illustrious and most ingenious nations of antiquity were weak and absurd. The Persians worshipped the sun; the Egyptians believed in an innumerable multitude of gods, and worshiped not only oxen, crocodiles, dogs, and cats, but even garlics and onions. The Greeks invented a political religion, and adored men and women, virtues and vices, air, water, and fire, and everything that vivid imagination could personify. Almost all the Greek philosophers reasoned and meditated upon the nature of the gods; but scarcely any of them reflected enough even to imagine that there was but one God, and not one of them ever conceived of him as the Creator of the world. Cicero has collected together all their opinions upon the nature of the gods, and pronounced them more like the dreams of madmen than sober judgment of wise men. In the first book of Ovid's *Metamorphoses*, there is an account of the change of chaos in the world. Before the sea, and the earth, and the sky that surrounds all things (says Ovid), there was a thing called chaos, and some of the gods (he does not know which), separated from each other the elements of this chaos, and turned them into the world; thus far and no farther could human reason extend. But the first words of the Bible are, "In the beginning God created the heavens and the earth." The blessed and sublime idea of God, as the creator of the universe, the source of all human happiness for which all the sages and philosophers of Greece and Rome groped in darkness and never found, is recalled in the first verse of the book of Genesis. I call it the source of all human virtue and happiness; because when we have attained the conception of a Being, who by the mere act of his will, created the world, it would follow as an irresistible consequence—even if we were not told that the same Being must also be the governor of his own creation—that man, with all other things, was also created by him, and must hold his felicity and virtue on the condition of obedience to his will. In the first chapters of the Bible there is a short and rapid historical narrative of the manner in which the world and man were made—of the condition upon which happiness and immortality were bestowed upon our first parents—of their transgression of this condition—of the punishment denounced upon them—and the promise of redemption from it by the "seed of the woman."

There are, and always have been, where the Holy Scriptures have been known, petty witlings and self-conceited reasoners, who cavil at some of the particular details of this narration. Even serious inquirers after truth have sometimes been perplexed to believe that there should have been evening and morning before the existence of the sun—that man should be made of clay, and woman from the ribs of man—that they should have been forbidden to eat an

apple, and for disobedience to that injunction, be with all
their posterity doomed to death, and that eating an apple
could give "the knowledge of good and evil"—that a
serpent should speak and beguile a woman. All this is
undoubtedly marvelous, and above our comprehension.
Much of it is clearly figurative and allegorical; nor is it easy
to distinguish what part of it is to be understood in a literal
and not in symbolical sense. But all that it imports us to
know or understand is plain; the great and essential
principles, upon which our duties and enjoyments depend,
are involved in no obscurity. A God, the Creator and
Governor of the universe, is revealed in all his majesty and
power; the terms upon which he gave existence and
happiness to the common parent of mankind are exposed to
us in the clearest light. Disobedience to the will of God was
the offence for which he was precipitated from paradise:
obedience to the will of God is the merit by which paradise
is to be regained. Here, then, is the foundation of all
morality—the source of all our obligations, as accountable
creatures. This idea of the transcendent power of the
Supreme Being is essentially connected with that by which
the whole duty of man is summed up; obedience to his will.
I have observed that natural reason might suffice for
obscure perception, but not for the clear discovery of these
truths. Even Cicero could start to his own mind the
question, whether justice could exist upon earth unless
founded upon piety, but could not settle it to his own
satisfaction. The ray of divine light contained in the
principle, that justice has no other foundation than piety,
could make its way to the soul of the heathen, but there it
was extinguished in the low, unsettled, and inconsistent

notions which were the only foundations of his piety. How could his piety be pure or sound, when he did not know whether there was one God or a thousand—whether he, or they had or had not any concern in the formation of the world, and whether they had any regard to the affairs or the conduct of mankind? Once assume the idea of a single God, the Creator of all things, whose will is the law of moral obligation to man, and to whom man is accountable, and piety becomes as rational as it is essential; it becomes the first of human duties; and not a doubt can henceforth remain, that fidelity in the associations of human piety, and that most excellent virtue, justice, repose upon no other foundation.

At a later age than Cicero, Longinus expressly quotes the third verse of the first chapter of Genesis as an example of the sublime. "And God said let there be light, and there was light;" and wherein consists its sublimity? In the image of the transcendent power presented to the mind, with the most striking simplicity of expression. Yet this verse only exhibits the effects of that transcendent power which the first verse discloses in announcing God as the Creator of the world. The true sublimity is in the idea given us of God. To such a God the heart of man must yield with cheerfulness the tribute of homage which it never could pay to the numerous gods of Egypt, to the dissolute debauchees of the heathen mythology, nor even to the more elevated, but not less fantastical imaginations of the Grecian philosophers and sages.

From your affectionate Father,

JOHN QUINCY ADAMS

LETTER III

The second general point of view, in which I propose for you to consider the Bible, to the end that it may "thoroughly furnish you unto all good works," is in the historical character.

To a man of liberal education, the study of history is not only useful, and important, but altogether indispensable, and with regard to the history contained in the Bible, the observation which Cicero makes respecting that of his own country is much more emphatically applicable, that "it is not so much praiseworthy to be acquainted with as it is shameful to be ignorant of it." History, so far as it relates to the actions and adventures of men, may be divided into five different classes. First, the history of the world, otherwise called universal history; second, that of particular nations; third, that of particular institutions; fourth, that of single families; and fifth, that of individual men. The last two of these classes are generally distinguished by the name of memoirs and biography. All these classes of history are to be found in the Bible, and it may be worth your while to discriminate them one from another. The universal history is short, and all contained in the first eleven chapters of Genesis, together with the first chapter of the first book of Chronicles, which is little more than a genealogical list of names; but it is of great importance, not only as it includes the history of the creation, of the fall of man, of the antediluvian world, and the flood by which the whole human race (excepting Noah and his family) were destroyed, but as it gives a very precise account of the time from the creation until the birth if Abraham. This is the foundation of ancient history, and in reading profane historians hereafter, I would advise you always to reflect upon their narratives with reference to it with respect to the chronology. A correct idea of this is so necessary to understand all history, ancient and modern, that I may hereafter write you something further concerning it: for the present I shall only recommend to your particular attention the fifth and eleventh chapters of Genesis, and request you to cast up and write me the amount of the age of the world when Abraham was born. The remainder of the book of Genesis, beginning at the twelfth chapter, is a history of one individual (Abraham) and his family during three generations of his descendants, after which the book of Exodus commences with the history of the same family, multiplied into a nation; this national and family history is continued through the books of the Old Testament until that of Job, which is of a peculiar character, differing in many particulars from every other part of the Scriptures. There is no other history extant which can give so interesting and correct view of the rise and progress of human associations, as this account of Abraham and his descendants, through all the vicissitudes to which individuals, families, and nations, are liable. There is no other history where the origin of a whole nation is traced up to a single man, and where a connected train of events and regular series of persons from generation to generation is preserved. As the history of a family, it is intimately connected with our religious principles and opinions, for it is the family from which (in his human character) Jesus Christ descended. It begins by relating the commands of God to Abraham, to abandon his country, his kindred, and his father's house; and to go to a land which he would show him. This command was accompanied by two promises; from which, and from their fulfillment arose the differences which I have just noticed between the history of the Jews and that of every other nation. The first of these promises was that "God would make Abraham a great nation and bless him;" the second, and incomparably the most important was, that "in him all the families of the earth should be blessed." This promise was made about two thousand years before the birth of Christ, and in him had its fulfillment. When Abraham, in obedience to the command of God, had gone into the land of Canaan, the Lord appeared unto him and made him a third promise, which was that he should give that land to a nation which should descend from him, as a possession: this was fulfilled between five and six hundred years afterward. In reading all the historical books of both the Old and the New Testament, as well as the books of the prophets, you should always bear in mind the reference which they have to these three promises of God to Abraham. All the history is no more than a narrative of the particular manner, and the detail of events by which those promises were fulfilled.

In the account of the creation, and the fall of man, I have already remarked that the moral doctrine inculcated by the Bible is, that the great consummation of all human virtue consists in obedience to the will of God. When we come hereafter to speak of the Bible in its ethical character, I shall endeavor to show you the intrinsic excellence of this principle; but I shall now only remark how strongly the principle itself is illustrated, first in the account of the fall, and next by the history of Abraham. In the account of the creation we are informed that God, after having made the world, created the first human pair, and "gave them dominion over every living thing that moveth upon the earth." He gave them also "every herb bearing seed, and the fruit of every tree for meat;" and all this we are told "God saw was very good." Thus the immediate possession of every thing was given them, and its perpetual enjoyment secured to their descendants, on condition of abstaining from the "fruit of the tree of knowledge of good and evil." It is altogether immaterial to my present remarks whether the narrative is to be understood in a literal or allegorical sense, as not only the knowledge, but the possession of created good was granted; the fruit of the tree, could confer upon them no knowledge but that of evil, and the command was nothing more than to abstain from that knowledge—to forbear from rushing upon their own destruction. It is not sufficient to say that this was a command in its own nature light and easy; it was a command to pursue the only law of their nature, to keep the happiness that had been heaped upon them without measure; but observe—it contained the principle of obedience—it was assigned to them as a duty— and the heaviest of penalties was denounced upon its transgression. They were not to discuss the wisdom, or justice of this command; they were not to inquire why it had been enjoined upon them, nor could they have the slightest possible motive for the inquiry: unqualified felicity and immortality were already theirs; wretchedness and death were alone forbidden them, but placed within their reach as merely trials of their obedience. They violated the law; they forfeited their joy and immortality; they "brought into the world, death, and all our wo [*sic*]." Here, then, is an extreme case in which the mere principle of obedience could be tried, and command to abstain from that from which every motive of reason and interest would have deterred had the command never been given—a command given in the easiest of all possible form, requiring not so much as an action of any kind, but merely forbearance; and its transgression was so severely punished, the only inference we can draw from it is that the most aggravated of all crimes, and that which includes in itself all others, is disobedience to the will of God.

Let us now consider how the principle of obedience is inculcated in the history of Abraham, by a case in the opposite extreme. God commanded Abraham to abandon for ever his country, his kindred, and his father's house, to go, he knew not where; promising, as a reward of his obedience, to bless him and his posterity, though he was then childless: he was required to renounce everything that could most contribute to the happiness and comfort of his life, and which was in his actual enjoyment; to become a houseless, friendless wanderer upon the earth, on the mere faith of the promise that a land should be shown him which his descendants should possess—that they should be a great nation—and that through them all mankind should receive in future ages a blessing. The obedience required of Adam, was merely to retain all the blessings he enjoyed; the obedience of Abraham was to sacrifice all that he possessed for the vague and distant prospect of a future compensation to his posterity: the self-control and self-denial required of Adam, was in itself the slightest that imagination can conceive—but its failure was punished by the forfeiture of all his enjoyments; the self-dominion to be exercised by Abraham was of the most severe and painful kind—but its accomplishment will ultimately be rewarded by the restoration of all that was forfeited by Adam. This restoration, however, was to be obtained by no ordinary proof of obedience; The sacrifice of mere personal blessing, however great, could not lay the foundation for the redemption of mankind from death; the voluntary submission of Jesus Christ to his own death, in the most excruciating and ignominious form, was to consummate the great plan of redemption, but the submission of Abraham to sacrifice his beloved, and only son Isaac—the child promised by God himself, and through whom all the greater promises were to be carried into effect, the feelings of nature, the parent's bowels, were all required to be sacrificed by Abraham to the blind unquestioning principle of obedience to the will of God. The blood of Isaac was not indeed shed—the butchery of an only son by the hand of his father, was a sacrifice which a merciful God did not require to be completely executed; but as an instance of obedience it was imposed upon Abraham, and nothing less than the voice of an angel from heaven could arrest his uplifted arm, and withhold him from sheathing his knife in the heart of his child. It was upon this testimonial of obedience, that God's promise of redemption was expressly renewed to Abraham: "In thy seed shall all the nations of the earth be blessed, because thou hast obeyed my voice."—Genesis xxii. 18.

LETTER IV

We were considering the Bible in its historical character, and as the history of a family. From the moment when the universal history finishes, that of Abraham begins, and thenceforth, it is the history of a family, of which Abraham is the first, and Jesus Christ the last person; and from the first appearance of Abraham, the whole history appears to have been ordered from age to age, expressly to prepare for the appearance of Christ upon earth. The history begins with the first and mildest trials of Abraham's obedience, and the promise as a reward of his fidelity, that "in him all the families of the earth should be blessed." The second trial, which required the sacrifice of his son, was many years afterward, and the promise was more explicit, and more precisely assigned as the reward of his obedience. There were between these periods, two intermediate occasions, recorded in the fifteenth and eighteenth chapters of Genesis—on the first of which, the word of the Lord came to Abraham in a vision, and promised him he should have a child, from whom a great

and mighty nation should proceed, which, after being in
servitude four hundred years in a strange land, should
become the possessors of the land of Canaan, from that of
Egypt, to the river Euphrates. On the second, the Lord
appeared to him and his wife, repeated the promise, that
they should have a child, that "Abraham should surely
become a great nation," and that "all the nations of the
earth should be blessed in him," "for I know him, saith the
Lord, that he will command his household after him, and
that they will keep the way of the Lord, to do justice and
judgment, that the Lord may bring upon Abraham that
which he hath spoken of him:" from all which it is obvious
that the first of the promises was made as subservient and
instrumental to the second—that the great and mighty
nation was to be raised as the means in the ways of God's
providence, for producing the sacred person of Jesus
Christ, through whom the perfect sacrifice of atonement
for the original transgression of man should be
consummated, and by which "all the families of the earth
should be blessed." I am so little versed in controversial
divinity, that I know not whether this eighteenth chapter of
Genesis, has ever been adduced in support of the doctrine
of Trinity; there is at least in it an alliteration of those divine
persons, and of one not little remarkable which I know not
how to explain; if taken in connection with the nineteenth,
it would seem that one of the men entertained by Abraham,
was God himself, and the other were angels, sent to destroy
Sodom.

Leaving this, however, let me ask your particular
attention, to the reason assigned by God for bestowing such

extraordinary blessings upon Abraham. It unfolds to us the
first and most important part of the superstructure of moral
principle, erected upon the foundation of obedience to the
will of God. The rigorous trials of Abraham's obedience
mentioned in this, and my last letter, were only tests to
ascertain his character in reference to the single, and I may
say abstract point of obedience. Here we have a precious
gleam of light, disclosing what the nature of this will of God
was, that he should command his children, and his
household after him; by which the parental authority to
instruct, and direct his descendants in the way of the Lord
was given him as an authority, and enjoined upon him as a
duty; and the lessons which he was then empowered and
required to teach his posterity were, "to do justice and
judgment." Thus, as obedience to the will of God, is the
first, and all-comprehensive virtue taught in the Bible, so
the second is justice and judgment toward mankind; and
this is exhibited as the result naturally following from the
other. In the same chapter is related the intercession of
Abraham with God for the preservation of Sodom from
destruction: the city was destroyed for its crimes, but the
Lord promised Abraham it should be spared, if only ten
righteous should be found in it: the principle of mercy was
therefore sanctioned in immediate connection with that of
justice. Abraham had several children; but the great
promise of God was to be performed through Isaac alone,
and of the two sons of Isaac, Jacob—the youngest—was
selected for the foundation of the second family and nation;
it was from Jacob that the multiplication of the family
began, and his twelve sons, were all included in the
genealogy of the tribes which afterward constituted the

Jewish people. Ishmael, the children of Keturah, and Esau, the eldest son of Isaac, were all the parents of considerable families, which afterward spread into nations; but they formed no part of the chosen people, and their history, with that of the neighboring nations, is only incidentally noticed in the Bible, so far as they had relations of intercourse or hostility with the people of God.

The history of Abraham and his descendants to the close of the book of Genesis is a biography of individuals: the incidents related of them are all the class belonging to domestic life. Joseph, indeed, became a highly distinguished public character in the land of Egypt, and it was through him that his father and all his brothers were finally settled there—which was necessary to prepare for the existence of their posterity as a nation, and to fulfil the purpose which God had announced to Abraham, that they should be four hundred years dwellers in a strange land. In the lives of Abraham, Isaac, Jacob, and Joseph, many miraculous events are recorded; but all those which are spoken of as happening in the ordinary course of human affairs have an air of reality about them which no invention could imitate. In some of the transactions related, the conduct of the patriarchs is highly blamable; circumstances of deep depravity are particularly told of Rueben, Simeon, Levi, and Judah, upon which it is necessary to remark that their actions are never spoken of with approbation, but always with strong marks of censure, and generally with a minute account of the punishment which followed upon their transgression. The vices and crimes of the patriarchs, are sometimes alleged as objections against the belief that persons guilty of them should ever have been especially favored by God; but, vicious as they were, there is every reason to be convinced that they were less so than their contemporaries: their vices appear to us at this day gross, disgusting and atrocious; but the written law was not then given, the boundaries between right and wrong were not defined with the same precision as in the tables given afterward to Moses; the law of nature was the only rule of morality by which they could be governed, and the sins of intemperance, of every kind recorded in Holy Writ, were at that period less aggravated than they have been in after ages, because they were in great measure sins of ignorance. From the time when the sons of Jacob were settled in Egypt until the completion of the four hundred years, during which God had foretold to Abraham that his family should dwell there, there is a chasm in the sacred history. We are expressly told that all the house of Jacob which came into Egypt, were threescore and ten: it is said then that Joseph died, as did all that generation; after which nothing further is related of their posterity than that "they were faithful and multiplied abundantly, and waxed exceeding mighty, and the land was filled with them, until there arose a new king who knew not Joseph."—On his first arrival in Egypt, Jacob had obtained a grant from Pharaoh of the land of Goshen, a place particularly suited to the pasturage of flocks: Jacob and his family were shepherds, and this circumstance was, in the first instance, the occasion upon which that separate spot was assigned to them, and, secondarily, was the means provided by God for keeping separate two nations thus residing together: every shepherd was an abomination to the Egyptians; and the Israelites were shepherds, although dwelling in the land of Egypt; therefore, the Israelites were sojourners and strangers; and by mutual antipathy toward each other, originating in their respective conditions, they were prevented from intermingling by marriage, and losing their distinctive characters. This was the cause which had been reserved by the Supreme Creator, during the space of three generations and more than four centuries, as the occasion for eventually bringing them out of the land; for, in proportion as they multiplied, it had the tendency to excite the jealousies and fears of the Egyptian king—as actually happened. These jealousies and fears suggested to him a policy of the most intolerable oppression and the most execrable cruelty toward the Israelites: not contented with reducing them to the most degraded condition of servitude, and making their lives bitter with hard bondage, he conceived the project of destroying the whole race, by ordering all the male children to be murdered as soon as they were born. In the wisdom of Providence, this very command was the means of preparing this family—when they had multiplied into a nation—for their issue from Egypt, and for their conquest of the land which had been promised to Abraham; and it was at the same time the immediate occasion of raising up the great warrior, legislator, and prophet, who was to be their deliverer and leader. Thenceforth, they are to be considered as a people, and their history as that of a nation. During a period of more than a thousand years, the Bible gives us a particular account of their destinies: an outline of their constitution, civil, military, and religious, with the code of laws presented to them by the Deity, is contained in the books of Moses, and will afford us copious materials for future consideration. Their subsequent revolutions of government under Joshua, fifteen successive chiefs denominated judges, and a succession of kings, until they were first dismembered into two separated kingdoms, and after a lapse of some centuries both conquered by the Assyrians and Babylonians, and at the end of seventy years partially restored their country and their temple, constitute the remaining historical books of the Old Testament, every part of which is full of instruction. But my present purpose is only to point your attention to their general historical character. My next will contain a few remarks on the Bible as a system of morals. In the meantime,

I remain your affectionate Father,

JOHN QUINCY ADAMS

LETTER V

In the promise with which my last letter to you upon the Bible was concluded, I undertook a task from the performance of which I have been hitherto deterred by its very magnitude and importance: the more I reflected upon the subject, the more sensible did I feel my incompetency to do it justice, and by a weakness too common in the world, from the apprehension of inability to accomplish as much as I ought, I have hitherto been withheld from the attempt to accomplish anything at all. Thus more than a year has elapsed, leaving me still burdened with the load of my promise; and in now undertaking to discharge it, I must promise that you are only to expect the desultory and undigested thoughts which I have not the means of combining into a regular and systematic work.

I shall not entangle myself in the controversy which has sometimes been discussed with a temper not very congenial to either the nature of the question itself or the undoubted principles of Christianity, whether the Bible, like all other systems of moralities, lays the ultimate basis of all human duties in self-love, or whether it enjoins duties on the principle of perfect, and disinterested benevolence. Whether the obligations are sanctioned by a promise of reward or a menace of punishment, the ultimate motive for its fulfillment may justly be attributed to selfish consideration. But if obedience to the will of God be the universal and only foundation of all moral duty, special injunctions may be binding upon the consciences of men, although their performance should not be secured either by the impulse of hope or fear. The law given from Sinai was a civil and municipal as well as a moral and religious code; it contained many statutes adapted to that time only, and to the particular circumstances of the nation to whom it was given; they could of course be binding upon them, and only upon them, until abrogated by the same authority which enacted them, as they afterward were by the Christian dispensation: but many others were of universal application—laws essential to the existence of men in society, and most of which have been enacted by every nation, which ever professed any code of laws. But the Levitical was given by God himself; it extended to a great varity of objects of infinite importance to the welfare of men, but which could not come within the reach of human legislation; it combined the temporal and spiritual authorities together, and regulated not only the actions but the passions of those to whom it was given. Human legislators can undertake only to prescribe the actions of men: they acknowledge their inability to govern and direct the sentiments of the heart; the very law styles it a rule of civil conduct, not of internal principles, and there is no crime in the power of an individual to perpetrate which he may not design, project, and fully intend, without incurring guilt in the eye of human law. It is one of the greatest marks of Divine favor bestowed upon the children of Israel, that the legislator gave them rules not only for action but for the government of the heart. There were occasionally a few short sententious principles of morality issued from the oracles of Greece; among them, and undoubted the most excellent of them, was that of self-knowledge, which one of the purest moralists and finest poets of Rome expressly says came from Heaven.

But if you would mark the distinguishing characteristic between true and false religion, compare the manner in which the ten commandments were proclaimed by the voice of the Almighty God, from Mount Sinai, with thunder, and lightning, and earthquake, by the sound of the trumpet, and in the hearing of six thousand souls, with the steadied secrecy, and mystery, and mummery, with which the Delphic and other oracle of the Grecian gods were delivered. The miraculous interposition of Divine power recorded in every part of the Bible, are invariably marked with grandeur and sublimity worthy of the Creator of the world, and before which the gods of Homer, not excepting his Jupiter, dwindle into the most contemptible pigmies; but on no occasion was the manifestation of the Deity so solemn, so awful, so calculated to make indelible impressions upon the imaginations and souls of the mortals to whom he revealed himself, as when he appeared in the character of their Lawgiver. The law thus dispensed was, however, imperfect; it was destined to be partly suspended

and improved into absolute perfection many ages afterward
by the appearance of Jesus Christ upon earth. But to judge
of its excellence as a system of laws, it must be compared
with human codes which existed or were promulgated at
nearly the same age of the world in other nations.
Remember, that the law was given 1,490 years before Christ
was born, at the time the Assyrian and Egyptian monarchies
existed: but of their government and laws we know scarcely
anything save what is collected from the Bible. Of the
Phrygian, Lydian, and Trojan states, at the same period,
little more is known. The president Gorget, in a very
elaborate and ingenious work on the origin of letters, arts,
and sciences, among the ancient nations, says, that "the
maxims, the civil and political laws of these people, are
absolutely unknown; that not even an idea of them can be
formed, with the single exception of the Lydians, of whom
Herodotus asserts, that their laws were the same as the
Greeks."—The same author contrasts the total darkness
and oblivion into which all the institutions of these mighty
empires have fallen, with the fulness [sic] and clearness and
admirable composition of Hebrew code, which has not only
descended to us entire, but still continues the national code
of the Jews (scattered as they are over the whole face of the
earth), and enters so largely into the legislation of almost
every civilized nation upon the globe. He observes that
"these laws have been prescribed by God himself: the
merely human laws of other contemporary nations can not
bear any comparison with them."

But my motive in forming the comparison, is to present
to your reflections as a proof—and to my mind a very

strong proof—of the reality of their divine origin: for how is it that the whole system of government, and administration, the municipal, political, ecclesiastical, military, and moral laws and institutions, which bound in society the numberless myriads [*sic*] of human beings who formed for many successive ages the stupendous monarchies of Africa and Asia, should have perished entirely and been obliterated from the memory of mankind, while the laws of a paltry tribe of shepherds, characterized by Tacitus, and the sneering infidelity of Gibbon, as "the most despised portion of their slaves," should not only have survived the wreck of those empires, but remain to this day rules of faith and practice to every enlightened nation of the world, and perishable only with it? The reason is obvious: it is their intrinsic excellence which has preserved them from the destruction which befalls all the works of mortal man. The precepts of the decalogue alone (says Gorget), disclose more sublime truths, more maxims essentially suited to the happiness of man, than all the writings of profane antiquity put together can furnish. The more you meditate on the laws of Moses, the more striking and brighter does their wisdom appear. It would be a laborious but not an unprofitable investigation, to reduce into a regular classification, like that of the institutes of Justinian or the Commentaries of Blackstone, the whole code of Moses, which embraces not only all the ordinary subjects of legislation together with the principles of religion and morality, but laws of ecclesiastical directions concerning the minutest actions and dress of individuals. This, however, would lead me too far from my present purpose, which is merely to consider the Bible as a system of morality; I shall therefore notice those parts of the law which may be referred particularly to that class, and at present must confine myself to a few remarks upon the decalogue itself, which, having been spoken by the voice, and twice written upon the stone tables by the finger of God, may be considered as the foundation of the whole system—of the ten commandments, emphatically so called, for the extraordinary and miraculous distinction by which they were promulgated.

The first four commandments are religious laws, fifth and tenth are properly and peculiarly moral and domestic rules; the other four are of the criminal department of municipal laws: the unity of the godhead, the prohibition of making graven images to worship; that of taking lightly (or in vain as the English translation expresses it) the name of the Deity, and the injunction to observe the Sabbath as a day sanctified and set apart for his worship, were all intended to inculcate the reverence for the one and only true God—that profound and penetrating sentiment of piety which, in a former letter, I urged as the great and only immovable foundation of all human virtue. Next to the duties toward the Creator, that of honoring the earthly parent is enjoined: it is to them that every individual owes the greatest obligations and to them that he is consequently bound by the first and strongest of all earthly ties. The following commands, applying to the relations between man and his fellow mortals, are all negative, as their application was universal, to every human being: it was not required that any positive acts of beneficence toward them should be performed; but only to abstain from wronging them, either: first, in their persons; second, in their property; third, in their conjugal rights; fourth, in their good name; after which all the essential enjoyments of life being thus guarded from voluntary injury, the tenth and closing commandment goes to the very source of all human actions—the heart—and positively forbids all those desires which first prompt and lead to every transgression upon the property and right of our fellow creatures. Vain, indeed, would be the search among the writings of profane antiquity (not merely of that remote and antiquity, but even in the most refined and philosophical ages of Greece and Rome), to find so broad, so complete and so solid a basis for morality as this decalogue lays down. Yet I have said it was imperfect—its sanctions, its rewards, its punishments, had reference only to present life, and it had no injunctions of positive beneficence toward our neighbors. Of these the law was not entirely destitute in its other parts; but, both in this respect and in the other, it was to be perfected by him who brought life and immortality to light in the gospel. Upon which subject you shall hear more,

From your affectionate Father,

JOHN QUINCY ADAMS

LETTER VI

I promised you, in my last letters, to state the particulars in which I deemed the Christian dispensation to be an improvement, or perfection of the law delivered at Sinai, considered as including a system of morality; but before I come to this point, it is proper to remark upon the character of the books of the Old Testament, subsequent to those of Moses. Some are historical, some prophetical, and some poetical; and two may be considered as peculiarly of the moral class—one being an affecting dissertation upon the vanity of human life, and another a collection of moral sentences under the name of Proverbs. I have already observed that the great immovable and eternal foundation of the superiority of scripture morals, to all other morality, was the idea of God disclosed in them and only in them: the unity of God, his omnipotence, his righteousness, his mercy, and the infinity of his attributes, are marked in every line of the Old Testament, in characters which nothing less than blindness, can fail to discern, and nothing less than fraud can misrepresent. This conception of God serving as a basis for the piety of his worshippers, was of course incomparably more rational and more profound, than it was possible that sentiment could be which adored devils for deities, or even that of philosophers, like Socrates, Plato, and Cicero, who with purer and more exalted ideas of the Divine nature, than the rabble of the poets, still considered the existence of any God at all, as a question upon which they could form no decided opinion. You have seen that even Cicero believed the only solid foundation of all human virtue to be piety; and it was impossible that a piety so far transcending that of all other nations should not contain in its consequences a system of moral virtue equally transcendent.

The first of the ten commandments was, that the Jewish people should never admit the idea of any other God—the object of the second, third, and fourth, was merely to impress with greater force the obligation of the first and to obviate the tendencies and temptations, which might arise to its being neglected, or disregarded. Throughout the whole law, the same injunctions are continually renewed; all the rites and ceremonies were adapted to root deeper into the hearts and souls of the chosen people, that the Lord Jehovah was to be for ever that sole and exclusive object of love. Reverence and adoration, unbounded as his own nature was the principle; every letter of the law, and the whole Bible is but a commentary upon it, and corollary from it. The law was given not merely in the form of a commandment from God, but in that of a covenant or compact between the Supreme Creator and the Jewish people; it was sanctioned by the blessing and the curse pronounced upon Mount Gerizim and Mount Ebal, in the presence of the whole Jewish people and strangers, and by the solemn acceptance of the whole people responding amen to every one of the curses denounced for violation on their part of the covenant. From that day until the birth of Christ (a period of about fifteen hundred years) the historical books of the Old Testament, are no more than a simple record of the fulfillment of the covenant, in all its blessings and curses, exactly adapted to the fulfillment or transgression of its duties by the people. The nation was first governed by Joshua, under the express appointment of God; then by a succession of judges, and afterward by a double line of kings, until conquered and carried into captivity by the kings of Assyria and Babylon: seventy years afterward restored to their country, their temple, and their laws; and again conquered by the Romans, and ruled by their tributary kings and proconsuls. Yet, through all their vicissitudes of fortune, they never complied with the duties to which they had bound themselves by the covenant, without being loaded with the blessings promised on Mount Gerizim, and never departed from them without being afflicted with some of the curses denounced upon Mount Ebal. The prophetical books are themselves historical—for prophecy, in the strictest sense, is no more than history related before the event; but the Jewish prophets (of whom there was a succession almost constant, from the time of Joshua to that of Christ) were messengers, specially commissioned of God, to warn the people of their duty, to foretell the punishments which awaited their transgressions, and finally to keep alive by uninterrupted prediction the expectation of the Messiah, "the seed of Abraham, in whom all the families of the earth should be blessed." With this conception of the Divine nature, so infinitely surpassing that of any other nation— with this system of moral virtue, so indissolubly blending as by the eternal constitution of things must be blended piety—with this uninterrupted series of signs and wonders, prophets and seers, miraculous interpositions of the omnipotent Creator, to preserve and vindicate the truth–it is lamentable; but to those who know the nature of man, it is not surprising to find the Jewish history little else than a narrative of idolatries and corruption of the Israelites and their monarchs. That the very people who had heard the voice of God from Mount Sinai, within forty days compel Aaron to make a golden calf, and worship that as the "God who brought them out of the land of Egypt"—that the very Solomon, the wisest of mankind, to whom God had twice revealed himself in visions—the sublime dictator of the temple, the witness, in the presence of the whole people, of the fire from heaven which consumed the offerings from the altar, and of the glory of the Lord that filled the house–that he, in his old age, beguiled by fair idolatresses, should have fallen from the worship of the everblessed Jehovah, to that of Ashtaroth and Milcom, &c., the abomination of all the petty tribes of Judea—that of Baal, and Dagon, &c., the sun, moon, and planets, and all the host of heaven—that the mountains and plains, every high place and every grove, should have swarmed with idols, to corrupt the hearts and debase the minds of a people so highly favored of Heaven, the elect of the Almighty—may be among the mysteries of Divine Providence, which it is not given to mortality to explain, but is inadmissible only to

those who presume to demand why it has pleased the
Supreme Arbiter of events, to create such a being as man.
Observe, however, that amid the atrocious crimes which
that nation so often polluted themselves with—through all
their servitudes, dismemberments, captivities, and
transmigrations—the Divine light, which had been
imparted exclusively to them, was never extinguished; the
law delivered from Sinai, was preserved in all purity; the
histories which attested its violations and its
accomplishments were recorded and never lost. The
writings of the prophets, of David, and Solomon, were all
inspired with the same idea of the Godhead, the same
intertwinement of religion and morality, and the same
anticipations of the divine, "Immanuel, the God with us;"
These survived all the changes of government and of
constitutions which befell the people: "The pillar of cloud
by day, and the pillar of fire by night,"—the law and the
prophets, eternal in their nature—went before them
unsullied, and unimpaired through all the ruins of rebellion
and revolution, of conquest and dispersion of war,
pestilence, and famine. The Assyrian, Babylonian, and
Egyptian empires, Tyre and Sidon, Carthage, and all the
other nations of antiquity, rose and fell in their religious
institutions at the same time as in their laws and
government: it was the practice of the Romans, when they
besieged a city, to invoke its gods to come over to them;
they considered the gods as summer friends, ready to desert
their votaries in the hour of calamity, or as traitors, ready to
sell them for a bribe; they had no higher estimate of their
own than of the stranger deities, whom, as Gibbon said—
"they were always ready to admit the freedom of the city."

All the gods of the heathens have perished with their makers; for where on the face of the globe, could now be found the being who believes in any one of them? So much more deep and strong was the hold which the God of Abraham, Isaac, and Jacob, took upon the imaginations and reason of mankind, that I might almost invert the question, and say, "Where is the human being found believing in any God at all, and not believing in him?"

The moral character of the Old Testament, then, is that piety to God is the foundation of all virtue, and the virtue is inseparable from it: but that piety without the practice of virtue is itself a crime and the aggravation of all iniquity. All the virtues which are here recognised by the heathen, are inculcated not only with more authority but with more energy of argument and more eloquent persuasion in the Bible than in all the writings of the ancient moralists. In one of the apocryphal books (Wisdom of Solomon), the cardinal virtues are expressly named; "If any man love righteousness, her labors are virtue, for she teacheth temperance, and prudence, and justice, and fortitude;" which are such things as men can have nothing more profitable in this life. The book of Job, whether considered as history or as an allegorical parable, was written to teach the lessons of patience under afflictions, of resignation under Divine chastisement, of undoubted confidence in the justice and goodness of God under every temptation or provocation to depart from it. The morality of the apocryphal books is generally the same as that of the inspired writers, except that in some of them there is more stress laid upon the minor objects of the law, and merely formal ordinances of police, and less continual recurrence to "the weightier matters."—The book of Ecclesiasticus, however, contains more wisdom than all the sayings of the seven Grecian sages. It was upon this foundation that the more perfect system of Christian morality was to be raised;—But I must defer the consideration to my next letter. In the meantime as I have urged that the scriptural idea of God is the foundation of all perfect virtue, and that it is totally different from the idea of God conceived by any ancient nation, I should recommend it to you in pursuing the Scriptures hereafter to meditate often upon the expressions by which they mark the character of the Deity, and to reflect upon the duties to him and to your fellow mortals which follow by the inevitable deductions from them. That you may have an exact idea of the opinions of ancient heathen philosophers concerning God, or rather the gods, study Cicero's dialogues, and read the abbe Olivet's remarks on the theology of the Grecian philosophers, annexed to his translations.

From your affectionate Father,

JOHN QUINCY ADAMS

LETTER VII

The imperfections of the Mosaic institution which it was the object of Christ's mission upon earth to remove, appear to me to have been these: First, The want of a sufficient sanction. The rewards and penalties of the Levitical law had all a reference to the present life. There are many passages in the Old Testament which imply a state of existence after death, and some which directly assert a future state of retribution; but none of these were contained in the delivery of the law. At the time of Christ's advent, it was so far from being a settled article of the Jewish faith, that it was a subject of bitter controversy between the two principal sects—of Pharisees who believed it and Sadducees who denied it. It was the special purpose of Christ's appearance upon earth, to bring immortality to light. He substituted the rewards and punishments of a future state of existence in the room of all others. The Jewish sanctions were exclusively temporal: those of Christ exclusively spiritual. Second, The want of universality. The Jewish dispensation was exclusively confined to a small and obscure nation. The purposes of the Supreme Creator in restricting the knowledge of himself to one petty herd of Egyptian slaves, are as inaccessible to our intelligence as those of his having concealed from them, and from the rest of mankind, the certain knowledge of their own immortality; yet the fact is unquestionable. The mission of Christ was intended to communicate to the whole human race all the permanent advantages of the Mosaic law, superadding to them—upon the condition of repentance—the kingdom of heaven, the blessing of eternal life. Third, the complexity of the objects of legislation. I have observed in a former letter, that the law from Sinai comprised, not only all the ordinary subjects of regulation for human societies, but those which human legislators can not reach. It was a civil law, a municipal law, an ecclesiastical law, a law of police, and a law of morality and religion: it prohibited murder, adultery, theft, and perjury; it prescribed rules for the thoughts as well as for the actions of men. The complexity, however practicable and even suitable for one small national society, could not have attained to all the families of the earth. The parts of the Jewish law adapted to promote the happiness of mankind, under every variety of situation and government in which they can be placed, were all recognised [sic] and adopted by Christ; and he expressly separated them from the rest. He disclaimed all interference with the ordinary objects of human legislation; he declared that his "kingdom was not of this world;" he acknowledged the authority of the Jewish magistrates; he paid for his own person the tribute to the Romans; he refused in more than one instance to assume the office of judge in matters of legal controversy; he strictly limited the object of his own precepts and authority to religion and morals; he denounced no temporal punishment; he promised no temporal reward; he took up man as a governable being, where the human magistrate is compelled to leave him, and supplied both precept of virtue and motive for practicing it, such as no other moralist or legislator ever attempted to introduce. Fourth, the burdensome duties of positive rites, minute formalities, and expensive sacrifices. All these had a tendency, not only to establish and maintain the separation of the Jews from all other nations, but in process of time had been mistaken by the scribes, and Pharisees, and lawyers, and probably by the body of the people, for the substance of religion. All the rites were abolished by Christ, or (as Paul expresses it) "were nailed to his cross." You will recollect that I am now speaking of Christianity, not as the scheme of redemption to mankind from the consequences of original sin, but as a system of morality for regulating the conduct of men while on earth; and the most striking and extraordinary feature of its character in this respect, is its tendency and exhortations to absolute perfection. The language of Christ to his disciples is explicit: "Be ye therefore perfect, even as your father in heaven is perfect"—and this he enjoins at the conclusion of that precept, so expressly laid down, and so unanswerably argued, to "love their enemies, to bless those who cursed them, and pray for those who despitefully used and persecuted them." He seems to consider the temper of benevolence in return for injury, as constituting of itself a perfection similar to that of the Divine nature. It is undoubtedly the greatest conquest which the spirit of man can achieve over its infirmities; and to him who can attain that elevation of virtue which it requires, all other victories over the evil passions must be comparatively easy. Nor was the absolute perfection merely preached by Christ as a doctrine: it was practised [sic] by himself throughout his life; practised [sic] to the last instant of his agony on the cross; practised [sic] under circumstances of trial, such as no other human being was ever exposed to. He proved by his own example the possibility of that virtue which he taught; and although possessed of miraculous powers sufficient to control all the laws of nature, he expressly and repeatedly declined the use of them to save himself from any part of the sufferings which he was able to endure.

The sum of Christian morality, then, consists in piety to God, and benevolence to man: piety, manifested, not by formal solemn rites and sacrifices of burnt-offerings, but by repentance, by obedience, by submission, by humility, by worship of the heart, and by benevolence; not founded upon selfish motives, but superior even to a sense of wrong, or the resentment of injuries. Worldly prudence is scarcely noticed among all the instructions of Christ: the pursuit of honors and riches, the objects of ambition and avarice, are strongly discountenanced in many places: and an undue solicitude about the ordinary cares of life is occasionally reproved. Of worldly prudence, there are rules enough in the Proverbs of Solomon, and in the compilations of the son of Sirach; Christ passes no censure upon them, but he left what I call the selfish virtues where he found them. It was not to proclaim common-place morality that he came down from Heaven; his commands were new; that his disciples should "love one another," that they should love even strangers, that they should "love their enemies." He prescribed barriers against all the maleficent [*sic*] passions; he gave us a law, the utmost point of perfection of which human powers are susceptible, and at the same time allowed degrees of indulgence and relaxation to human frailty, proportioned to the power of any individual. An eminent writer in support of Christianity (Dr. Paley) expresses the opinion, that the direct object of the Christian revelation was to supply motives, and not rules—sanctions, and not precepts; and he strongly intimates that, independent of the purpose of Christ's atonement and propitiation for the sins of the world, the only object of his mission upon earth was to reveal a future state, "to bring life and immortality to light." He does not appear to think that Christ promulgated any new principle of morality; and he positively asserts that "morality, neither in the gospel nor in any other book, can be a subject of discovery, because qualities of actions depend entirely on their effects, must all along have been the subjects of human experience." To this I reply in the express words of Jesus: "A new commandment I give you, that ye love one another;" and I add, that this command explained, illustrated, and dilated, as it was by the whole tenor of his discourses, and especially by the parable of the good Samaritan, appears to me to be not only entirely new, but, in the most rigorous sense of the word, a discovery in morals; and a discovery, the importance of which to the happiness of the human race, as far exceeds any discovery in the physical laws of nature, as the soul is superior to the body. If it be objected that the principles of benevolence toward enemies, and the forgiveness of injuries, may be found not only in the Old Testament, but even in some of the heathen writers, particularly the discoveries of Socrates, I answer, that the same may be said of the immortality of the soul, and of the rewards and punishments of a future state. The doctrine was no more a discovery than the precept; but their connexion [*sic*] with each other, the authority with which they were taught, and the miracles by which they were enforced, belong exclusively to the mission of Christ. Attend particularly to the miracle recorded in the second chapter of Luke, as having taken place at the birth of Jesus; when the angel of the Lord said to the shepherds: "Fear not, for behold I bring you glad tidings of great joy, which shall be to all people; for unto you is born this day in the city of David, a Savior, who is Christ the Lord." In these words the character of Jesus, as a Redeemer, was announced; but the historian adds—"And suddenly there was with the angel a multitude of the heavenly host praising God and singing, glory to God in the highest, and on earth peace, good will toward men." These words, as I understand them, announced the moral precept of benevolence as explicitly for the object of Christ's appearance, as the preceding words had declared the purpose of redemption. It is related in the life of the Roman dramatic poet, Terence, that when one of the personages of his comedy, the "Self-Tormentor," the first time uttered on the stage the line "Homo sum, humani nil alienum puto" (I am a man, nothing human is uninteresting to me), a universal shout of applause burst forth from the whole audience, and that in so great a multitude of Romans, and deputies from the nations, their subjects and allies, there was not one individual but felt in his heart this noble sentiment. Yet how feeble and defective it is, in comparison

with the Christian command of charity as unfolded in the
discoveries of Christ and enlarged upon in the writings of
his apostles. The heart of man will always respond with
rapture to this sentiment when there is no selfish or
unsocial passion to oppose it: but the command to lay it
down as the great and fundamental rule of conduct for
human life, and to subdue and sacrifice all the tyrannical
and selfish passion to preserve it, this is the peculiar and
unfading glory of Christianity; this is the conquest over
ourselves, which, without the aid of a merciful God, none
of us can achieve, and which it was worthy of his special
interposition to enable us to accomplish.

From your affectionate Father,

JOHN QUINCY ADAMS

LETTER VIII

The whole system of Christianity appears to have been set forth by its Divine Author in his sermon on the mount, recorded in the fifth, sixth, and seventh chapters of Matthew. I intend hereafter to make them the subject of remarks, much more at large; for the present, I confine myself merely to general views. What I would impress upon your mind, is infinitely important to the happiness and virtue of your life, as the general spirit of Christianity, and the duties which result from it. In my last letter, I showed you, from the very words of our Savior, that he commanded his disciples to aim at absolute perfection, and that this perfection consisted in self-subjugation and brotherly love, in the complete conquest of our own passions, and in the practice of benevolence to our fellow creatures. Among the Grecian systems of moral philosophy, that of the Stoics resembles the Christian doctrine in the particular of requiring the total subjugation of the passions; and this part of the Stoic principles was adopted by the academies. You will find the question discussed with all the eloquence and ingenuity of Cicero, in the fourth of his Tusculan disputations, which I advise you to read and meditate upon. You will there find proved, the duty of subduing the passions. It is sometimes objected that this theory is not adapted to the infirmities of human nature; that it is not made for a being so constituted as man; that an earthen vessel is not formed to dash itself against a rock; that in yielding to the impulses of the passions, man only follows the dictates of his nature; that to subdue them entirely, is an effort beyond his powers. The weakness and frailty of our nature, it is not possible to deny—it is too strongly tested by all human experience, as well as by the whole tenor of the Scriptures; but the degree of weakness must be measured by the efforts to overcome it, and not by indulgence to it. Once admit weakness as an argument to forbear exertion, and it results in absolute impotence. It is also very inconclusive reasoning to infer, that because perfection is not absolutely to be obtained, it is therefore not to be sought. Human excellence consists in approximation to perfection: and the only means of approaching to any term, is by endeavoring to obtain the term itself. With these convictions upon the mind—with a sincere and honest effort to practise [sic] upon them, and with the aid of a divine blessing, which is promised to it, the approaches to perfection may at least be so great, as to nearly answer all the ends which absolute perfection itself could attain. All exertion, therefore, is virtue; and if the tree be judged by its fruit, it is certain that all the most virtuous characters of heathen antiquity, were the disciples of the Stoic doctrine. But let it even be admitted that a perfect command of the passions is unattainable to human infirmity, it will still be true, that the degree of moral excellence possessed by any individual, is in exact proportion to the degree of control he exercises over himself. According to the Stoics, all vice was resolvable into folly: according to the Christian principle it is all the effect of weakness. In order to preserve the dominion of our own passions, it behooves us to be constantly and strictly on our guard against the influence and infection of the passions of others. This caution above all is necessary to youth; and I deem it indispensable to enjoin it upon you—because, as kindness and benevolence comprise the whole system of Christian duties, there may be, and often is, great danger of falling into errors and vice, merely for the want of energy to resist the example or enticement of others. On this point the true character of Christian morality appears to me to have been misunderstood by some of its ablest and warmest defenders.

In Paley's "View of the Evidences of Christianity," there is a chapter upon the morality of the gospel, the general tenor, of which (as of the whole work) is excellent, but in which there is the following passage: "There are two opposite descriptions of character, under which mankind may generally be classed: the one possesses vigor, firmness, resolution, is active and daring, quick in its sensibilities, jealous of its fame, eager in its attachments, inflexible of its purposes, violent in its resentment; the other meek, yielding, complying, forgiving, not prompt to act, but willing to suffer, silent and gentle under rudeness and insults, suing for reconciliation, where others would demand satisfaction; giving away to the pushes of impudence, conceding and indulgent to the prejudices, the wrong-headedness, the intractability of others, with whom it has to deal. The former of these characters is, and ever has been, the favorite of the world; it is the character of great men—there is a dignity in it which commands respect. The latter is poor-spirited, tame, and abject. Yet, so it has happened, that with the founder of Christianity, the latter is the subject of his commendation, his precepts, his example, and that the former is so in no part of its composition. Dr. Paley in this place adopts the opinion of Soame Jennings, whose essay on the "Internal Evidences of Christianity" he strongly recommends; but I can not consider it either as an accurate and discerning delineation of character, nor as exhibiting a correct representation of Christian principles. The founder of Christianity did indeed pronounce distinct and positive blessings upon the "poor in spirit," which is by no means synonymous with the "poor-spirit;" and upon the meek; but in what part of the gospel did Dr. Paley find him countenancing by "commendation, by precept or example, the tame and abject"? The character which Christ assumed upon earth, was that of a Lord and Master; it was in that character his disciples received and acknowledged him. The obedience he required was unbounded, infinitely beyond that which was ever claimed by the most absolute earthly sovereign of his subjects: never for one moment did he recede from this authoritative station; he preserved it in washing the feet of his disciples; he preserved it in answer to the officer who struck him for this very deportment to the high-priest; he preserved it in the agony of his ejaculation on the cross, "Father, forgive them, for they know not what they do." He expressly declared himself, "the Prince of this world, and the Son of God." He spoke as one having authority, not only to his disciples, but to his mother, to his judges, to Pilate the Roman governor, to John the Baptist, his precursor; and there is not in the four gospels, one act, not one word recorded of him (excepting his communion with God), that was not a direct or implied assertion of authority. He said to his disciples, "Learn of me, for I am meek and lowly of heart," &c.; but where did he ever say to them, "Learn of me, for I am tame and abject"? There is certainly nothing more strongly marked in the precepts and examples of Christ, than the principle of stubborn and inflexible resistance against the impulses of others to evil. He taught his disciples to renounce everything that is counted enjoyment upon earth; "to take up their cross," and to suffer ill-treatment, persecution, and death, for his sake. What else is the book of the "Acts of the Apostles," than a record of the faithfulness with which these chosen ministers of the gospel carried these injunctions in to execution? In the conduct and speeches of Peter, John, and Paul, is there anything that could justly be called "tame or abject"? Is there anything indicating a resemblance to the second class of character into which Dr. Paley divides all mankind? If there is a character upon historical record distinguished by a bold, inflexible, tenacious, and intrepid spirit, it is that of Paul. It was to such characters only, that the commission to "teach all nations," could be committed with certainty of success. Observe the impression of Christ, in his charge to Peter (a rock): "And upon this rock I will build my church, and the gates of hell shall not prevail against it." Dr. Paley's Christian is one of those drivellers, who, to use a vulgar phrase, can never say no, to anybody. The true Christian is the "Justum et tenacem propositi virum" of Horace, ("the man who is just and steady to his purpose"). The combination of these qualities so essential to heroic character, with those of meekness, lowliness of heart, and brotherly love, is what constitutes that moral perfection of which Christ gave an example in his own life, and to which he commands his disciples to aspire. Endeavor, my dear son, to discipline your heart, and to govern your conduct by these principles thus combined; be meek, be gentle, be kindly affectionate to all mankind, not excepting your enemies; but never be "tame or abject;" never give way to the pushes of impudence, or show yourself yielding or complying to prejudice, wrong-headedness, or intractability, which would lead or draw you astray from the dictates of your own conscience, and your own sense of right: "till you die, let not your integrity depart from you:" build your house upon the rock, and then let the rains descend, and the floods come, and the winds blow and beat upon the house—"it shall not fall, it will be founded upon a rock." So promises your blessed Lord and Master, and so prays your affectionate Father.

JOHN QUINCY ADAMS

LETTER IX

The fourth and last point of view in which I proposed to offer you some general observations upon the Scriptures, was with reference to literature; and the first remark that presents itself is, that the five books of Moses, are the most ancient monuments of written language now extant in the world; the book of Job is nearly of the same date, and by many of the Jewish and Christian commentators, is thought to have been written by Moses. The employment of alphabetical characters to represent all the articulations of the human voice, is the greatest invention that ever was compassed by human genius. Plato says that "it was the discovery of either a God, or a man divinely inspired." The Egytians ascribed it to Thot [*sic*], whom the Greeks afterward worshiped under the name of Hermes. This is, however, a fabulous origin. That it was an Egyptian invention, there is little doubt; and it was a part of that learning of the Egyptians, in all of which we are told, "Moses was versed." It is probable that when Moses wrote, this act was, if not absolutely recent, of no very remote invention. There was but one copy of the law written in a book. It was deposited in the ark of the covenant, and was read aloud once in seven years, to all the people, at their general assembly in the feast of tabernacles. There was one other copy of the law, written upon stone, erected on Mount Ebal. It does not appear that there existed any other copies. In process of time the usage of reading it thus must have been dropped, and the monument upon Mount Ebal must have perished; for in the reign of Josiah, about eight hundred years afterward, the book of the law was found in the temple. How long it had been lost is not expressly told; but from the astonishment and consternation of Josiah upon hearing the book read, its contents must have been long forgotten so that scarcely a tradition of them remained. We are indeed told, that, when the ark of the covenant was deposited in the temple of Solomon, there was nothing in the ark save the two tables, which Moses put therein at Horeb. The two tables contained not the whole law, but the ten commandments: the book of the law was therefore no longer in the ark, at the dedication of Solomon's temple; that is, about five hundred years after the law was given, and three hundred before that book was found by Hezekiah the high-priest, in the eighteenth year of Josiah. From these circumstances, as well as from the expedients used by Moses and Joshua for preserving the ceremonial law, and the repeated covenant between God and the people, it is observed that the art and practice of writing was extremely rare, and that very few of the people were even taught to read; that there were few books extant, and of those few, only single copies; the art of writing, speaking, and thinking, with their several modifications of grammar, rhetoric, and logic, were never cultivated among the Hebrews, as they were (though not till a thousand years later than Moses) among the Greeks. Philosophical research and the spirit of analysis appear to have belonged among the ancient nations, exclusively to the Greeks; they studied language as a science, and from the discoveries they made in this pursuit, resulted a system of literary compositions, founded upon logical deductions. The language of the ancient writers was not constructed upon the foundation of abtruse [sic] science; it partakes of the nature of all primitive languages, which is almost entirely figurative; and in some degree of the character of primitive writing and hieroglyphics. We are not told from what materials Moses compiled the book of Genesis (which contains the history of the creation, and of three hundred years succeeding it, and which terminates three generations prior to the birth of Moses himself), whether he had it altogether from tradition, or whether he collected it from the more ancient written or printed memorials. The account of the creation, of the fall of man, and all the antediluvian part of the history, carries strong internal evidences of having been copied or (if I may express myself) translated from hieroglyphic or symbolical record; the story is of the most perfect simplicity, the discourses of the persons introduced, are given as if taken down verbatim, from their mouths, and the narrative is scarcely anything more than the connecting link of the discourses; the genealogies are given with great precision; and, this is one of the most remarkable peculiarities of the Old Testament; the rest is all figurative ; the rib, the garden, the tree of life, and of the knowledge of good and evil, the apple, the serpent, are all images which seem to indicate a hieroglyphic origin. All the historical books, of both the Old and New Testaments, retain the peculiar characteristics that I have noticed; the simplicity and brevity of the narrative, the practice of repeating all discourses in the identical words spoken, and the constant use of figurative symbolical and allegorical language. But of the rules of composition, prescribed by the Grecian schools, the unities of Aristotle, or the congruities of figures taught by the Greek philologists, not a feature is to be seen. The Psalms are a collection of songs; the Song of Solomon is pastoral poem; the Proverbs are a collection of moral sentences and maxims, apparently addressed by Solomon to his son, with the addition of others of the same description; the prophetical books are partly historical and partly poetical— they contain the narrative of visions and relations of the Deity to the prophets, who recorded them.

In the New Testament, the four gospels and the Acts of the Apostles are historical—they contain memoirs of the life of Christ, and some of his disciples, and the proceedings of some of his principal apostles, for some years after his decease. The simplicity of the narrative, is the same as that of the Old Testament; the style in general, indicates an age when reading and writing, had become more common, and books more multiplied. The Epistles of Paul, are the productions of a mind educated in the learning of the age, and well versed in the Grecian literature; from his history, it appears that he was not only capable of maintaining an argument with the doctors of the Jewish law, but of discussing principles with the Stoic and Epicurean philosophers; his speech at Athens is a specimen of eloquence worthy of an audience in the native country of Demosthenes. The Apocalypse of John resembles, in many respects, some of the prophetical books of the Old Testament; the figurative, symbolical, and allegorical language of these books shows a range of imagination suitable only to be the record of dreams and visions—their language is in many parts inexplicably obscure. It has been, and it is to this day, among the follies and vices of many sects of Christians, to attempt explanations of them, adapted to sectarian purposes and opinions. The style of none of the books, of either the Old or New Testament, affords a general model for imitation to a writer of the present age; the principles and rules for composition derived from Greek and Roman schools, and the example of their principal writers, have been so generally adopted in modern literature, that the Scriptures—differing so essentially from them—could not be imitated without great affectation; but for pathos of narrative; for the selections of incidents that go directly to the heart; for the picturesque of character and manner; the selection of circumstances that mark the individuality of persons; for copiousness, grandeur, and sublimity of imagery; for unanswerable cogency and closeness of reasoning; and for irresistible force of persuasion: no book in the world deserves to be so unceasingly studied, and so profoundly meditated upon as the Bible.

I shall conclude here the series of letters which I proposed, about two years ago, to write you for the purpose of exhorting you to search the Scriptures, and of pointing out to your considerations the general points of application; with a view to which, I thought this study might be made profitable to the improvement and usefulness of your future life. There are other and particular points to which I may hereafter occasionally invite your attention. I am sensible how feeble and superficial what I have written has been, and every letter has convinced me more and more of my own incompetence to the adequate performance of the task I had assumed; but my great object was to show you the importance of devoting your own faculties to this pursuit; to read the Bible is of itself a laudable occupation and can scarcely fail of being a useful employment of time; but the habit of reflecting upon what you have read is equally essential as that of reading itself, to give it all the efficacy of which it is susceptible. I therefore recommend to you to set apart a small portion of every day to read one or more chapters of the Bible, and always read it with reference to some particular train of observation or reflection. In these letters, I have suggested to you four general ones. Considering the Scriptures as Divine Revelations; as historical records; as a system of morals; and as literary composition. There are many other points of view in which they may be subjects of useful investigation. As an expedient for fixing your attention, make it also a practice for some time, to minute down in writing your reflections upon what you read from day to day; you may perhaps at first find this irksome, and your reflections scanty and unimportant, but they will soon become both easy and copious. Be careful of all not to let your reading make you a pedant, or a bigot; let it never puff you up with pride or a conceited opinion of your own knowledge, nor make you intolerant of the opinions which others draw from the same source, however different from your own. And may the merciful Creator, who gave the Scriptures for our instruction, bless your study of them, and make them to you "fruitful of good works." Your affectionate Father,

JOHN QUINCY ADAMS

THE WANTS OF MAN

By John Quincy Adams

In 1840, Mr. Morgan, the present secretary of state of New York, occupied a seat in Congress next to that of Mr. Adams. Several young ladies in Mr. Ogle's district had requested Mr. Adams' autograph. In complying with that request, Mr. Adams added the following poem, a copy of which Mr. Morgan obtained. Mr. Adams, be it remembered, when this spirited poem was written, had attained his 74th year.

"Man wants but little here below,
Nor wants that little long."

Goldsmith's Hermit

I.

"Man wants but little here below,
Nor wants that little long."
'Tis not with me exactly so—
But 'tis so in the song.
My wants are many, and, if told,
Would muster many a score;
And were each wish a mint of gold,
I still should long for more.

II.

What first I want is daily bread,
And canvas-backs and wine,
And all the realms of nature spread
Before me when I dine:
Four courses scarcely can provide
My appetite to quell,
With four choice cooks from France beside,
To dress my dinner well.

III.

What next I want, at heavy cast,
Is elegant attire—
Black sable furs for winter's frost,
And silks for summer's fire,
And Cashmere shawls and Brussels lace
My bosom's front to deck,
And diamond rings my hands to grace,
And rubies for my neck.

IV.

And then I want a mansion fair,
A dwelling-house in style,
Four stories high, for wholesome air,
A massive marble pile:
With halls for banquets and for balls
All furnished rich and fine;
With stabled studs in fifty stalls,
And cellars for my wine.

V.

I want a garden and a park
My dwelling to surround—
A thousand acres (bless the mark!)
With walls encompassed round,
Where flocks may range and herds may low,
And kids and lambkins play—
And flowers and fruits commingled grow
All Eden to display.

VI.

I want, when summer's foliage falls,
And autumn strips the trees,
A house within the city's walls,
For comfort and for ease—
But here, as space is somewhat scant,
And acres rather rare,
My house in town I only want
To occupy—a square.

VII.

I want a steward, butler, cooks,
A coachman, footman, grooms,
A library of well-bound books,
And picture-garnished rooms—
Correggios, Magdalen, and Night,
The Matron of the chair—
Guido's fleet-courses in their flight,
And Claudes, at least a pair.

VIII.

I want a cabinet profuse
Of medals, coins, and gems;
A printing-press, for private use,
Of fifty thousand ems,
And plants, and minerals, and shells—
Worms, insects, fishes, birds,
And every beast on earth that dwells
In solitude or herds.

IX.

I want a board of burnished plate,
Of silver and of gold—
Tureens of twenty pounds in weight,
With sculpture's richest mould—
Plateaus with chandeliers and lamps,
Plates, dishes, all the same,
And porcelain vases with the stamps
Of Sevres, Angouleme.

X.

And maples of fair glossy stain
Must form my chamber-doors,
And carpets of the Wilton grain
Must cover all my floors;
My walls with tapestry bedecked
Must never be outdone,
And damask curtains must protect
their colors from the sun.

XI.

And mirrors of the largest pane
From Venice must be brought,
And sandal-wood and bamboo-cane
For chairs and tables bought;
On all the mantelpieces, clocks
Of thrice-gilt bronze must stand,
And screens of ebony and box
Invite the stranger's hand.

XII.

I want—(who does not want?)—a wife,
Affectionate and fair,
To solace all the woes of life,
And all its joys to share—
Of temper sweet, of yielding will,
Of firm yet placid mind—
With all my faults to love me still,
With sentiment refined.

XIII.

And as Time's car incessant runs,
And Fortune fills my store,
I want of daughters and of sons
From eight to half a score:
I want (alas! Can mortal dare
Such bliss on earth to crave?)
That all the girls be chaste and fair—
The boys all wise and brave.

XIV.

And when my bosom's darling sings
With melody divine,
A pedal-harp of many strings
Must with her voice combine:
A piano, exquisitely wrought,
Must open stand, apart,
That all my daughters may be taught
To win the stranger's heart.

XV.

My wife and daughters will desire
Refreshment from perfumes,
Cosmetic for the skin require,
And artificial blooms:
The civet, fragrance shall dispense
And treasured sweets return—
Cologne revive the flagging sense,
And smoking amber burn.

XVI.

And when, at night, my weary head
Begins to droop and doze,
A southern chamber holds my bed
For nature's soft repose:
With blankets, counterpanes, and sheet,
Mattress and bed of down,
And comfortables for my feet,
And pillows for my crown.

XVII.

I want a warm and faithful friend
To cheer the adverse hour,
Who ne'er to flatter will descend
Nor bend the knee to power—
A friend to chide me when I'm wrong,
My inmost soul to see,
And that my friendship proves as strong
For him as his for me.

XVIII.

I want a kind and tender heart
For others' wants to feel,
A soul secure from Fortune's dart,
And bosom armed with steel—
To bear divine chastisement's rod,
And mingling, in my plan,
Submission to the will of God
With charity to man.

XIX.

I want a keen, observing eye—
An ever-listening ear,
The truth through all disguise to spy,
And wisdom's voice to hear:
A tongue to speak at virtue's need,
In Heaven's sublimest strain,
And lips the cause of man to plead,
And never plead in vain.

XX.

I want uninterrupted health
Throughout my long career;
And streams of never-failing wealth
To scatter far and near,
The destitute to cloth and feed,
Free bounty to bestow—
Supply the helpless orphan's need and
sooth the widow's wo.

XXI.

I want the genius to conceive,
The talents to unfold
Designs, the vicious to retrieve—
The virtuous to uphold:
Inventive power, combining skill,
A persevering soul,
Of human hearts to mould the will
And reach from pole to pole.

XXII.

I want the seals of power and place,
The ensigns of command—
Charged by the people's unbought grace,
To rule my native land:
Nor crown, nor scepter, would I ask,
But from my country's will,
By day, by night, to ply the task
Her cup of bliss to fill.

XXIII.

I want the voice of honest praise
To follow me behind,
And to be thought in future days
The friend of human kind—
That after-ages, as they rise,
Exulting may proclaim,
In choral union to the skies,
Their blessings on my name.

XXIV.

These are the wants of mortal man:
I can not want them long,
For life itself is but a span
And earthly bliss a song.
My last great want, absorbing all,
Is, when beneath the sod,
And summoned to my final call,
The mercy of my God.

XXV.

And oh! While circles in my veins
Of life the purple stream,
And yet a fragment small remains
Of nature's transient dream,
My soul, in humble hope unscarred,
Forget not thou to pray,
That this thy want may be prepared
To meet the judgment-day!

THE END